The Fourth Dimension

P. D. Ouspensky

Kessinger Publishing's Rare Reprints

Thousands of Scarce and Hard-to-Find Books on These and other Subjects!

- Americana
- Ancient Mysteries
- Animals
- Anthropology
- Architecture
- Arts
- Astrology
- Bibliographies
- Biographies & Memoirs
- Body, Mind & Spirit
- Business & Investing
- Children & Young Adult
- Collectibles
- Comparative Religions
- Crafts & Hobbies
- Earth Sciences
- Education
- Ephemera
- Fiction
- Folklore
- Geography
- Health & Diet
- History
- Hobbies & Leisure
- Humor
- Illustrated Books
- Language & Culture
- Law
- Life Sciences
- Literature
- Medicine & Pharmacy
- Metaphysical
- Music
- Mystery & Crime
- Mythology
- Natural History
- Outdoor & Nature
- Philosophy
- Poetry
- Political Science
- Science
- Psychiatry & Psychology
- Reference
- Religion & Spiritualism
- Rhetoric
- Sacred Books
- Science Fiction
- Science & Technology
- Self-Help
- Social Sciences
- Symbolism
- Theatre & Drama
- Theology
- Travel & Explorations
- War & Military
- Women
- Yoga
- *Plus Much More!*

We kindly invite you to view our catalog list at:
http://www.kessinger.net

THIS ARTICLE WAS EXTRACTED FROM THE BOOK:

New Model of the Universe

BY THIS AUTHOR:

P. D. Ouspensky

ISBN 0766108228

READ MORE ABOUT THE BOOK AT OUR WEB SITE:

http://www.kessinger.net

OR ORDER THE COMPLETE
BOOK FROM YOUR FAVORITE STORE

ISBN 0766108228

Because this article has been extracted from a parent book, it may have non-pertinent text at the beginning or end of it.

Any blank pages following the article are necessary for our book production requirements. The article herein is complete.

CHAPTER II

THE FOURTH DIMENSION

The idea of hidden knowledge—The problem of the invisible world and the problem of death—The invisible world in religion, in philosophy, in science—The problem of death and various interpretations of it—The idea of the fourth dimension—Various approaches to it—Our position in relation to the "domain of the fourth dimension"—Methods of studying the fourth dimension—Hinton's ideas—Geometry and the fourth dimension—Morosoff's article—An imaginary world of two dimensions—The world of perpetual miracle—The phenomena of life—Science and unmeasurable phenomena—Life and thought—Perception of plane beings—A plane being's different stages of understanding the world—Hypothesis of the third dimension—Our relation to the "invisible"—The world of the unmeasurable round us—Unreality of bodies of three dimensions—Our own fourth dimension—Deficiency of our perception—Properties of perception in the fourth dimension—Inexplicable phenomena of our world—The psychic world and attempts to interpret it—Thought and the fourth dimension—Expansion and contraction of bodies—Growth—The phenomena of symmetry—Diagrams of the fourth dimension in Nature—Movement from the centre along radii—The laws of symmetry—States of matter—Relation of time and space in matter—Theory of dynamic agents—Dynamic character of the universe—The fourth dimension within us—The "Astral sphere"—Hypothesis of fine states of matter—Transformation of metals—Alchemy—Magic—Materialisation and dematerialisation—Prevalence of theories and absence of facts in astral hypotheses—Necessity for a new understanding of "space" and "time".

THE idea of the existence of a hidden knowledge, surpassing all the knowledge a man can attain by his own efforts, must grow and strengthen in people's minds from the realisation of the insolubility of many questions and problems which confront them.

Man may deceive himself, may think that his knowledge grows and increases, that he knows and understands more than he knew and understood before, but sometimes he may be sincere with himself and see that in relation to the fundamental problems of existence he is as helpless as a savage or a little child, although he has invented many clever machines and instruments which have complicated his life but have not rendered it any more comprehensible.

Speaking still more sincerely with himself man may recognise that all his scientific and philosophical systems and theories are similar to these machines and implements, for they only serve to complicate the problems without explaining anything.

Among the insoluble problems with which man is surrounded, two occupy a special position—the problem of the invisible world and the problem of death.

In all the history of human thought, in all the forms, without exception, which this thought has ever taken, people have always divided the world into the *visible* and the *invisible*; and they have always understood that the visible world accessible to their direct observation and study represents something very small, perhaps even something non-existent, in comparison with the enormous invisible world.

Such an assertion, that is, that the division of the world into the visible and the invisible has existed always and everywhere, may appear strange at first, but in reality all existing general schemes of the world, from the most primitive to the most subtle and elaborate, divide the world into the visible and the invisible and can never free themselves from this division. This division of the world into the visible and the invisible is the foundation of man's thinking about the world, no matter how he names or defines this division.

The fact of such a division becomes evident if we try to enumerate the various systems of thinking of the world.

First of all let us divide all the systems of thinking of the world into three categories:

1. Religious systems.
2. Philosophical systems.
3. Scientific systems.

All religious systems without exception, from those theologically elaborated down to the smallest details, such as Christianity, Buddhism, Judaism, to the completely degenerated religions of "savages", appearing as "primitive" to modern knowledge, invariably divide the world into visible and invisible. In Christianity: God, angels, devils, demons, souls of living and dead people, heaven or hell. In paganism: gods personifying forces of nature, thunder, sun, fire, spirits of mountains, woods, lakes, water-spirits, house spirits—all this is the invisible world.

In philosophy there is the world of events and the world of causes, the world of things and the world of ideas, the world of phenomena and the world of noumena. In Indian philosophy, especially in certain schools of it, the visible or phenomenal world, that is Maya or illusion, which means a wrong conception of the invisible world, does not exist at all.

In science, the invisible world is the world of small quantities and, strange though it is, also the world of large quantities. The visibility of the world is determined by the scale. The invisible world is on the one hand the world of micro-organisms, cells, the microscopic and the ultra-microscopic world; still further it is the world of molecules, atoms, electrons, "vibrations"—and, on the other hand, the world of invisible stars, other solar systems, unknown universes. The microscope expands the limits of our vision in one direction, the telescope in the other. But both increase visibility very little in comparison with what remains invisible. Physics and chemistry show us the possibility of investigating phenomena in such small quantities or in such distant worlds as will never be visible to us. But this only strengthens the fundamental idea of the existence of an enormous, invisible world round the small, visible world.

Mathematics goes even farther. It calculates such relations of magnitudes and such relations between these relations as have nothing similar in the visible world surrounding us. And we are forced to admit that the invisible world differs from the visible not only in size, but in some other properties which we can neither define nor understand and which only show us that laws, inferred by us for the visible world, cannot refer to the invisible world.

In this way invisible worlds, the religious, the philosophical, and the scientific, are, after all, more closely related to one another than they would at first appear. And these invisible worlds of different categories possess identical properties common to all. These properties are, first: incomprehensibility for us, that is, incomprehensibility from the ordinary point of view, or for ordinary means of cognition; and, second: the fact that they contain the causes of the phenomena of the visible world.

This idea of causes is always associated with the invisible world. In the invisible world of the religious systems, invisible forces govern people and visible phenomena. In the scientific invisible world the causes of visible phenomena always come from the invisible world of small quantities and " vibrations ". In the philosophical systems the phenomenon is only our conception of the noumenon, that is, an illusion, the real cause of which remains hidden and inaccessible to us.

This shows that on all levels of his development man has always understood that the causes of visible and observable phenomena lie beyond the sphere of his observation. He has found that among observable phenomena certain facts could be regarded as causes of other facts, but these deductions were insufficient for the explanation of *everything* that occurred in himself and around him. Therefore in order to be able to explain the causes it was necessary for him to have an invisible world consisting either of " spirits ", or " ideas ", or " vibrations ".

The other problem which attracted the attention of men by its insolubility and which by the form of its approximate solution determined the direction and development of human thought, was the problem of death, that is, the explanation of death, the idea of future life, of the immortal soul, or the absence of the immortal soul, and so on.

Man could never reconcile himself to the idea of death as disappearance. Too many things contradicted it. There were in himself too many traces of the dead, their faces, words, gestures, opinions, promises, threats, the feelings which they roused, fear, jealousy, desire. All these continued to live in him, and the fact of their death was more and more forgotten. A man saw his dead friend or enemy in his dreams. He appeared exactly as he was before. Evidently he was living *somewhere*, and could come *from somewhere* by night.

So it was very difficult to believe in death and man always needed theories for the explanation of the existence after death.

On the other hand, echoes of esoteric teachings on life and death sometimes reached man. He could hear that the visible, earthly, observable, life of man is only a small part of the life belonging to him. And man of course understood in his own way these fragments which reached him, changed them in his own fashion, adapted them to his own level and understanding, and built out of them some theory of future existence, similar to existence on the earth.

The greater part of religious teachings on the future life connect it with the idea of reward or punishment, sometimes in an undisguised, sometimes in a veiled form. Heaven and hell, transmigration of souls, reincarnation, the wheel of lives—all these theories contain the idea of reward or punishment.

But religious theories often do not satisfy man, and in addition to the recognised, orthodox, ideas of life after death there usually exist other, as it were illegitimate, ideas of the world beyond the grave or of the spirit-world, which allow a greater freedom of imagination.

No religious teaching, no religious system, can by itself satisfy people. There is always some other, more ancient system of popular belief underlying it or hiding behind it. Behind external Christianity, behind external Buddhism, there stand the remains of ancient pagan creeds (in Christianity the remains of pagan beliefs and customs, in Buddhism " the cult of the devil "), which sometimes make a deep mark on the external religion. In modern Protestant countries, for instance, where the remains of ancient paganism are already completely extinct, there have come into existence, under the outward mask of logical and moral Christianity, systems of primitive thinking of the world beyond the grave, such as spiritualism and kindred teachings.

And theories of existence beyond the grave are always connected with theories of the invisible world; the former are always based upon the latter.

THE FOURTH DIMENSION

This all relates to religion and "pseudo-religion". There are no philosophical theories of existence beyond the grave. All theories of life after death can be called religious or, more correctly, pseudo-religious.

Moreover, it is difficult to take philosophy as a whole, so diverse and contradictory are the various speculative systems. Still, to a certain extent, it is possible to accept as a standard of philosophical thinking the view which can see the unreality of the phenomenal world and the unreality of man's existence in the world of things and events, the unreality of the separate existence of man and the incomprehensibility for us of the forms of real existence, although this view can be based on very different foundations, either materialistic or idealistic. In both cases the question of life and death acquires a new character and cannot be reduced to the naïve categories of ordinary thinking. For such a view there is no particular difference between life and death, because, strictly speaking, for it there are no proofs of a separate existence, of separate lives.

There are not and there cannot be any *scientific* theories of existence after death because there are no facts in favour of the reality of such an existence, while science, successfully or unsuccessfully, wishes to deal with facts. In the fact of death the most important point for science is a certain change in the state of the organism, which stops all vital functions, and the decomposition of the body following upon it. Science sees in man no psychic life independent of the vital functions, and all theories of life after death, from the scientific point of view, are pure fiction.

Modern attempts at "scientific" investigation of spiritualistic phenomena and similar things lead nowhere and can lead nowhere, for there is a mistake here in the very setting of the problem.

In spite of the difference between the various theories of the future life, they all have one common feature. They either picture the life beyond the grave as similar to the earthly life, or deny it altogether. They do not and cannot attempt to conceive life after death in new forms or new categories. And this is precisely what makes all usual theories of life after death unsatisfactory. Philosophical and strictly scientific thought shows us the necessity of reconsidering the problem from completely new points of view. A few hints coming from the esoteric teaching partly known to us indicate the same.

It already becomes evident that if the problem of death and life after death can be approached in any way, it must be approached from quite a new angle. In the same way, the question of the invisible world must also be approached from a new angle. All we know, all we have thought till now, shows us the reality and the vital importance of these problems. Until he has answered in one way or another the questions of the invisible world and of life after death, man cannot think of anything else without creating a whole series of contradictions. Right or wrong, man must build for himself some kind of explanation. And he must base his treatment of the problem of death either upon science, or upon religion, or upon philosophy.

But to a thinking man both the "scientific" denial of the possibility of life after death and the pseudo-religious admission of it (for we know nothing but pseudo-religion), and also different spiritualistic, theosophical and similar theories, quite justly appear equally naïve.

Nor can the abstract philosophical view satisfy man. Such a view is too remote from life, too remote from direct, real sensations. One cannot live by it. In relation to the phenomena of life and their possible causes, unknown to us, philosophy is very like astronomy in its relation to the distant stars. Astronomy calculates the movement of stars which are at colossal distances from us. But all celestial bodies are alike for it. They are nothing but moving dots.

Thus, philosophy is too remote from concrete problems such as the problem of future life. Science does not know the world beyond the grave; pseudo-religion creates the other world in the image of the earthly world.

This helplessness of man in the face of the problems of the invisible world and of death becomes particularly obvious when we begin to realise that the world is far bigger and far more complex than we have hitherto thought, and that what we think we know occupies only a very insignificant place amidst that which we do not know.

Our basic conception of the world must be broadened. Already we feel and know that we can no longer trust the eyes with which we see, or the hands with which we touch. The real world eludes us at such attempts to ascertain its existence. A more subtle method, a more efficient means, are needed.

The ideas of the "fourth dimension", ideas of "many dimensional space", show the way by which we may arrive at the broadening of our conception of the world.

The expression "fourth dimension" is often met with in conversational language and in literature, but it is very seldom that anybody has a clear idea of what it really means. Generally the fourth dimension is used as the synonym of the mysterious, miraculous, "supernatural", incomprehensible and incognisable, as a kind of general definition of the phenomena of the "super-physical" world.

"Spiritualists" and "occultists" of various schools often make use of this expression in their literature, assigning to the sphere of

THE FOURTH DIMENSION

the fourth dimension all the phenomena of the "world beyond" or the "astral sphere". But they do not explain what it means, and from what they say one can understand only that the chief property which they ascribe to the fourth dimension is "unknowableness".

The connecting of the idea of the fourth dimension with existing theories of the invisible world or the world beyond is certainly quite fantastic, for, as has already been said, all religious, spiritualistic, theosophical and other theories of the invisible world first of all make it exactly similar to the visible and consequently "three-dimensional" world.

Therefore mathematics quite justly objects to the established view of the fourth dimension as something belonging to the "beyond".

The very idea of the fourth dimension must have arisen in close connection with mathematics, or, to put it better, in close connection with the idea of measuring the world. It must have arisen from the supposition that, besides the three known dimensions of space—length, breadth and height—there might also exist a fourth dimension, inaccessible to our perception.

Logically, the supposition of the existence of the fourth dimension can be based on the observation of those things and events in the world surrounding us for which the measurement in length, breadth and height is not sufficient, or which elude all measurement; because there are things and events the existence of which calls for no doubt, but which cannot be expressed in any terms of measurement. Such are, for instance, various effects of vital and psychic processes; such are all ideas, mental images and memories; such are dreams. If we consider them as existing in a real, objective sense, we can suppose that they have some other dimension besides those accessible for us, that is, some extension immeasurable for us.

There exist attempts at a purely mathematical definition of the fourth dimension. It is said for instance: "In many problems of pure and applied mathematics formulæ and mathematical expressions are met with containing four or more variable quantities, each of which, independently of the others, may be positive or negative and lie between $+ \infty$ and $- \infty$. And as every mathematical formula, every equation, can have a dimensional expression, so from this is deduced an idea of space which has four or more dimensions".[1]

The weak point of this definition is the proposition accepted as unquestionable that every mathematical formula, every equation, can have a dimensional expression. In reality such a proposition is entirely without ground, and this deprives the definition of all meaning.

---

[1] The article "Four-dimensional space" in the Russian Encyclopedia of Brockhaus and Efron.

In reasoning by analogy with the existing dimensions, it must be supposed that if the fourth dimension existed it would mean that side by side with us lies some other space which we do not know, do not see, and into which we are unable to pass. It would then be possible to draw a line from any point of our space into this "domain of the fourth dimension" in a direction unknown to us and impossible either to define or to comprehend. If we could visualise the direction of this line going out of our space then we should see the "domain of the fourth dimension".

Geometrically this proposition has the following meaning. We can conceive simultaneously three lines perpendicular and not parallel to one another. These three lines are used by us to measure the whole of our space, which is therefore called three-dimensional. If the "domain of the fourth dimension" lying outside our space exists, this means that besides the three perpendiculars known to us, determining the length, the breadth and the height of solids, there must also exist a fourth perpendicular, determining some new extension unknowable to us. Then the space measurable by these four perpendiculars could be called four-dimensional.

We are unable to define geometrically, or to conceive, this fourth perpendicular, and the fourth dimension still remains extremely enigmatic. The opinion is sometimes met with that mathematicians know something about the fourth dimension which is inaccessible to ordinary mortals. Sometimes it is said, and one can even find such assertions in literature, that Lobatchevsky "discovered" the fourth dimension. During the last twenty years the discovery of the "fourth dimension" has often been ascribed to Einstein or Minkovsky.

In reality mathematics can say very little about the fourth dimension. There is nothing in the hypothesis of the fourth dimension that would make it inadmissible from a mathematical point of view. This hypothesis does not contradict any of the accepted axioms and, because of this, does not meet with particular opposition on the part of mathematics. Mathematicians even admit the possibility of establishing the relationship that should exist between four-dimensional and three-dimensional space, i.e. certain properties of the fourth dimension. But they do all this in a very general and rather indefinite form. No exact definition of the fourth dimension exists in mathematics.

Lobatchevsky actually treated the geometry of Euclid, i.e. geometry of three-dimensional space, as a particular case of geometry, which ought to be applicable to a space of any number of dimensions. But this is not mathematics in the strict sense of the word; it is only metaphysics on mathematical themes, and the deductions from it cannot be formulated mathematically or can be formulated only in specially constructed expressions, which have no general meaning.

Other mathematicians regarded axioms accepted in the geometry of Euclid as artificial and incorrect, and attempted to disprove them on the strength, chiefly, of certain deductions from Lobatchevsky's spherical geometry, and to prove, for instance, that parallel lines meet. They contended that the accepted axioms are correct only for three-dimensional space, and on the basis of their arguments, which disproved these axioms, they built up a new geometry of many dimensions.

But all this is not geometry of four dimensions.

The fourth dimension could only be considered as geometrically proved when the direction of the unknown line starting from any point of our space and going into the region of the fourth dimension could be determined, i.e. when a means of constructing a fourth perpendicular is found.

It is difficult to describe even approximately the significance which the discovery of the fourth perpendicular in our universe would have for our knowledge. The conquest of the air; hearing and seeing at a distance; establishing connections with other planets or with other solar systems; all this is nothing in comparison with the discovery of a new dimension. But so far it has not been made. We must recognise that we are helpless before the riddle of the fourth dimension, and we must try to examine the problem within the limits accessible to us.

After a closer and more exact investigation of the problem itself we come to the conclusion that it cannot be solved in existing conditions. The problem of the fourth dimension, though purely geometrical at the first glance, cannot be solved by geometrical means. Our geometry of three dimensions is as insufficient for the investigation of the question of the fourth dimension as planimetry alone is insufficient for the investigation of questions of stereometry. We must find the fourth dimension, if it exists, in a purely experimental way, and also find a means for a projective representation of it in three-dimensional space. Only then shall we be able to create geometry of four dimensions.

Even slight acquaintance with the problem of the fourth dimension shows the necessity for studying it from the psychological and physical sides.

The fourth dimension is unknowable. If it exists and if at the same time we cannot know it, that evidently means that something is lacking in our psychic apparatus, in our faculties of perception; in other words, phenomena of the region of the fourth dimension are not reflected in our organs of sense. We must examine why this should be so, what are our defects on which this non-receptivity depends, and must find the conditions (even if only theoretically) which would make the fourth dimension comprehensible and accessible to us. These are all questions relating to psychology or, possibly, to the theory of knowledge.

Further, we know that the region of the fourth dimension (again, if it exists) is not only unknowable for our psychic apparatus, but is *inaccessible* in a purely physical sense. This must depend not on our defects, but on the particular properties and conditions of the region of the fourth dimension itself. It is necessary to examine what these conditions are, which make the region of the fourth dimension inaccessible to us, and to find the relation between the physical conditions of the region of the fourth dimension and the physical condition of our world. And having established this, it is necessary to see whether in the world surrounding us there is anything similar to these conditions, that is, whether there are any relations analogous to relations between the region of three dimensions and that of four dimensions.

Speaking in general, before attempting to build up a geometry of four dimensions it is necessary to create a physics of four dimensions, that is, to find and to define physical laws and conditions which may exist in the space of four dimensions.

Many people have worked at the problem of the fourth dimension. Fechner wrote a great deal about the fourth dimension. From his discussions about worlds of one, two, three and four dimensions there follows a very interesting method of investigating the fourth dimension by means of building up analogies between worlds of different dimensions, i.e. between an imaginary world on a plane and the three-dimensional world, and between the three-dimensional world and the world of four dimensions. This method is used by nearly all those who have ever studied the problem of higher dimensions, and we shall have occasion to meet with it further on.

Professor Zöllner evolved the theory of the fourth dimension from observations of " mediumistic " phenomena, chiefly of phenomena of so-called " materialisation ". But his observations have long been considered doubtful because of the established fact of the insufficiently strict arrangement of his experiments (Podmore and Hislop).

A very interesting summary of almost all that has ever been written about the fourth dimension up to the nineties of last century is to be found in the books of C. H. Hinton. These books contain also many of Hinton's own ideas; but, unfortunately, side by side with the valuable ideas there is a great deal of unnecessary dialectic such as always accumulates round the question of the fourth dimension.

Hinton makes several attempts at a definition of the fourth dimension from the physical side, as well as from the psychological. Considerable space is occupied in his books by the description of a method, invented by him, of accustoming the mind to cognition of the fourth dimension. It consists of a long series of exercises for the perceiving and the visualising apparatus, with sets of differently coloured cubes, which are meant to be memorised, first in one position, then in another, then in a third, and after that to be visualised in different combinations.

The fundamental idea which guided Hinton in the creation of this method of exercises is that the awakening of " higher consciousness " requires the " casting out of the self " in the visualisation and cognition of the world, i.e. the accustoming of oneself to know and conceive the world, not from a personal point of view (as we generally know and conceive it), but as it is. For this it is necessary, first of all, to learn to visualise things not as they appear to us, but as they are, even if only in a geometrical sense; from this there must develop the capacity to know them, i.e. to see them, as they are, also from other points of view besides the geometrical.

The first exercise suggested by Hinton consists in the study of a cube composed of 27 smaller cubes coloured differently and bearing definite names. After having thoroughly learned the cube made up of smaller cubes, it has to be turned over and learned and memorised in the reverse order. Then the position of the smaller cubes has to be changed and memorised in that order, and so on. As a result, according to Hinton, it is possible to cast out in the cube studied the concepts " up and down ", " right and left ", and so on, and to know it independently of the position with regard to one another of the smaller cubes composing it, i.e. probably to visualise it simultaneously in different combinations. This would be the first step towards casting out the self-elements in the conception of the cube. Further on, there is described an elaborate system of exercises with series of differently coloured and differently named cubes, out of which various figures are composed. All this has the same purpose, to cast out the self-elements in the percepts and in this way to develop higher consciousness.

Casting out the self-elements in percepts, according to Hinton's idea, is the first step towards the development of higher consciousness and towards the cognition of the fourth dimension.

He says that if there exists the capacity of vision in the fourth dimension, that is, if we are able to see objects of our world as if from the fourth dimension, then we shall see them, not as we see them in the ordinary way, but quite differently.

We usually see objects as either above or below us, or on the same level with us, to the right or to the left, behind us or in front of us, and always from one side only—the one facing us—and in perspective. Our eye is an extremely imperfect instrument; it gives us an utterly incorrect picture of the world. What we call perspective is in reality a distortion of visible objects which is produced by a badly constructed optical instrument—the eye. We see all objects distorted. And we visualise them in the same way. But we visualise them in this way entirely owing to the habit of seeing them distorted, that is, owing to the habit created by our defective vision, which has weakened the capacity of visualisation.

But, according to Hinton, there is no necessity to visualise objects of the external world in a distorted form. The power of visualisation is not limited by the power of vision. We see objects distorted, but we know them as they are. And we can free ourselves from the habit of visualising objects as we see them, and we can learn to visualise them as we know they really are. Hinton's idea is precisely that before thinking of developing the capacity of seeing in the fourth dimension, we must learn to visualise objects as they would be seen from the fourth dimension, i.e. first of all, not in perspective, but from all sides at once, as they are known to our " consciousness ". It is just this power that should be developed by Hinton's exercises. The development of this power to visualise objects from all sides at once will be the casting out of the self-elements in mental images. According to Hinton, " casting out the self-elements in mental images must lead to casting out the self-elements in perceptions ". In this way, the development of the power of visualising objects from all sides will be the first step towards the development of the power of seeing objects as they are in a geometrical sense, i.e. the development of what Hinton calls a " higher consciousness ".

In all this there is a great deal that is right, but also a great deal that is arbitrary and artificial. First of all, Hinton does not take into consideration the difference between the various psychic types of men. A method that may prove satisfactory for himself may produce no results or even contrary results for other people. Second, the very psychological foundation of his system of exercises is too unstable. Usually he does not know when to stop, carries his analogies too far and in that way deprives many of his conclusions of all value.

From the point of view of geometry, according to Hinton, the question of the fourth dimension may be examined in the following way.

We know geometrical figures of three kinds:
Figures of one dimension—lines.

THE FOURTH DIMENSION

Figures of two dimensions—planes.

Figures of three dimensions—solids.

A line is regarded here as the trace of a point moving in space. A plane—as the trace of a line moving in space. A solid—as the trace of a plane moving in space.

Let us imagine a straight line limited by two points, and let us designate this line by the letter a. Let us imagine this line a moving in space in a direction perpendicular to itself and leaving a trace of its movement. When it has traversed a distance equal to its length, the trace left by it will have the form of a square, the sides of which are equal to a line a, i.e. a^2.

Let us imagine this square moving in space in a direction perpendicular to two of its adjoining sides and leaving a trace of its movement. When it has traversed a distance equal to the length of one of the sides of the square, its trace will have the form of a cube, i.e. a^3.

Now if we imagine the movement of a cube in space, what form will the trace left by such a movement, i.e. figure a^4, assume?

Examining the correlations of figures of one, two and three dimensions, i.e. lines, planes and solids, we can deduce the rule that a figure of a higher dimension can be regarded as the trace of the movement of a lower dimension.

On the basis of this rule we may regard figure a^4 as the trace of the movement of a cube in space.

But what is this movement of a cube in space, the trace of which becomes a figure of four dimensions?

If we examine the way in which figures of higher dimensions are constructed by the movement of figures of lower dimensions, we shall discover several common properties and several common laws in these formations.

In fact, when we consider a square as the trace of the movement of a line, we know that all the points of this line have moved in space; when we consider a cube as the trace of the movement of a square, we know that all the points of the square have moved. Moreover, the line moves in a direction perpendicular to itself; the square in a direction perpendicular to two of its dimensions.

Consequently, if we consider the figure a^4 as the trace of the movement of a cube in space, we must remember that all the points of the given cube have moved in space. Moreover, we may deduce from analogy with the above that the cube was moving in space in a direction which is not contained in the cube itself, i.e. a direction perpendicular to its three dimensions. This direction, then, would be the fourth perpendicular unknown to us in our space and in our geometry of three dimensions.

Further, we may determine a line as an infinite number of points; a square as an infinite number of lines; a cube as an infinite number of squares. By analogy with this we may determine the figure a^4 as an infinite number of cubes.

Further, looking at the square we see nothing but lines; looking at the cube we see its surfaces, or possibly even only one of its surfaces.

It is quite possible that the figure a^4 would appear to us as a cube. To put it in a different way, the cube is what we see of the figure a^4.

Further, a point may be determined as a cross-section of a line; a line as a cross-section of a surface; a surface as a cross-section of a solid; a three-dimensional body can therefore be determined as a cross-section of a four-dimensional body.

Generally speaking, in every four-dimensional body we shall see its three-dimensional projection or section. A cube, a sphere, a pyramid, a cone, a cylinder, may be projections or cross-sections of four-dimensional bodies unknown to us.

In 1908 I came across a curious article on the fourth dimension (in Russian) published in the review *Sovremenny Mir*.

It was a letter written by N. A. Morosoff[1] in 1891 to his fellow-prisoners in the fortress of Schlüsselburg. It is of interest chiefly because it contains, in a very picturesque form, an exposition of the fundamental proposition of the method of reasoning about the fourth dimension by means of analogies, which was mentioned above.

The first part of Morosoff's article is very interesting, but in his final conclusions as to what may exist in the domain of the fourth dimension he deviates from the method of analogies and assigns to the fourth dimension the "spirits" which spiritualists evoke in their séances. And then, having denied the existence of spirits, he denies also the objective meaning of the fourth dimension.

---

[1] N. A. Morosoff, a scientist by education, belonged to the revolutionary parties of the seventies and eighties. He was arrested in connection with the murder of the Emperor Alexander II and spent twenty-three years in prisons, chiefly in the fortress of Schlüsselburg. Liberated in 1905 he wrote several books, one on the Revelation of St. John, another on Alchemy, on Magic, etc., which found fairly numerous readers in the period before the War. It was rather curious that the public liked in Morosoff's books not what he actually wrote, but what he wrote about. His real intentions were very limited and in strict accordance with the scientific ideas of the seventies. He tried to present "mystical subjects" rationally; for instance, he explained the Revelation as nothing but a description of a thunderstorm. But being a good writer, Morosoff gave a very vivid exposition of his themes, and sometimes he added little-known material. So his books produced a quite unexpected result, and many people became interested in mystical subjects and in mystical literature after reading Morosoff's books. After the revolution, Morosoff joined the Bolsheviks and remained in Russia. Although, as far as is known, he has not taken part in destructive work himself, he has written nothing more and on solemn occasions expresses his official admiration of the Bolshevik régime. (Note to the translation.) P. O.

THE FOURTH DIMENSION

It is generally supposed that fortress walls do not exist in the fourth dimension, and that was probably the reason why the fourth dimension was one of the favourite subjects of the conversations held at Schlüsselburg by means of tapping.

N. A. Morosoff's letter is an answer to the questions put to him in one of these conversations. He writes:

My dear friends, our short Schlüsselburg summer is nearing its end, and the dark mysterious autumn nights are coming. In these nights, spreading like a black cloak over the roof of our prison and enveloping with impenetrable darkness our little island with its old towers and bastions, it would seem that the shadows of our friends and predecessors who perished here flit invisibly round about these walls, look at us through the windows and enter into mysterious communication with us who still live. And we ourselves, are we not but shadows of what we used to be? Are we not transformed into some kind of tapping spirits, conversing unseen with one another through the stone walls which divide us, like those that perform at spiritualistic séances.

All day long I have thought of your discussion of to-day about the fourth, the fifth and other dimensions of the space of the universe which are inaccessible to us. With all my power I have tried to imagine at least the fourth dimension of the world, the one in which, as metaphysicians affirm, everything that is under lock and key may suddenly appear open, and in which all confined spaces can be entered by beings able to move not only along our three dimensions, but also along the fourth, to which we are unaccustomed.

You ask me for a scientific examination of the problem. Let us speak first of the world of only two dimensions; and later we will see whether it will give us the possibility of drawing certain conclusions about different worlds.

Let us take a certain plane—for instance, that which separates the surface of Lake Ladoga which surrounds us, from the atmosphere above it, in this quiet autumn evening. Let us suppose that this plane is a separate world of two dimensions, peopled with its own beings, which can move only on this plane, like the shadows of swallows and sea-gulls flitting in all directions over the smooth surface of the water which surrounds us, but remains for ever hidden from us behind these battlements.

Let us suppose that, having escaped from behind our Schlüsselburg bastions, you went for a bathe in the lake.

As beings of three dimensions you also have the two dimensions which lie on the surface of the water. You will occupy a definite place in the world of shadow beings. All the parts of your body above and below the level of the water will be imperceptible to them, and they will be aware of nothing but your contour, which is outlined by the surface of the lake. Your contour must appear to them as an object of their own world, only very astonishing and miraculous. The first miracle from their point of view will be your sudden appearance in their midst. It can be said with full conviction that the effect you would create would be in no way inferior to the unexpected appearance among ourselves of some ghost from the unknown world. The second miracle would be the surprising changeability of your external form. When you are immersed up to your waist your form will be for them almost elliptical, because only the line on the surface surrounding your waist and impenetrable for them will be perceptible to them. When you begin to swim you will assume in their eyes the outline of a man. When you wade into a shallow place so that the surface on which they live will encircle your legs, you will appear to them transformed into two ring-shaped beings. If, desirous of keeping you in one place, they surround you on all sides, you can step over them and find yourselves free from them in a way quite inconceivable to them. In their eyes you would be all-powerful beings—inhabitants of a higher world, similar to those supernatural beings about whom theologians and metaphysicians tell us.

Now if we suppose that apart from these two worlds, the plane world and the world we live in, there exists a world of four dimensions, superior to ours, it will become clear that in relation to us its inhabitants would be exactly the same as we are in relation to the inhabitants of a plane. They must appear in our midst in the same unexpected way and disappear from our world at their will, moving along the fourth or some other higher dimension.

In a word the analogy, so far, is complete. Further we shall find in the same analogy a complete refutation of all our hypotheses.

If indeed the beings of the four-dimensional world were not purely our invention, their appearance in our midst would be an ordinary, everyday occurrence.

Further Morosoff discusses whether we have any reason to suppose that "supernatural beings" really exist, and he comes to the conclusion that we have no grounds for such a hypothesis unless we are prepared to believe in fairy-tales.

The only indication, worthy of our attention, of the existence of such beings can be found, according to Morosoff, in the teachings of spiritualism. But his own experience in "spiritualism" convinced him that in spite of the strange phenomena that undoubtedly occur at spiritualistic séances, "spirits" take no part in them. So-called "automatic writing", usually cited as a proof of the co-operation of intelligent forces of another world at these séances, is, according to his observations, a result of thought-reading. Consciously or unconsciously a "medium" "reads" the thoughts of those present and from these thoughts obtains the answers to their questions. Morosoff attended many séances, but never met with a case where there was anything in the answers received which was not known to any of the people present, or where answers were in a language unknown to any present. Therefore, though not doubting the sincerity of the majority of spiritualists, Morosoff concludes that "spirits" have nothing to do with phenomena at séances.

His experience of spiritualism, he says, had finally convinced him many years previously that the phenomena which he assigned to the fourth dimension do not really exist. He says that at such spiritualistic séances answers are given unconsciously by the actual people present and that therefore all suppositions concerning the existence of the fourth dimension are pure imagination.

These conclusions of Morosoff are quite unexpected, and it is difficult to understand how they were arrived at. Nothing can be said against his opinion of spiritualism. The psychic side of spiritualistic phenomena is undoubtedly quite " subjective ". But it is quite incomprehensible why Morosoff sees the " fourth dimension " in spiritualistic phenomena alone and why, denying the " spirits ", he denies the fourth dimension. This looks like a ready-made solution offered by that official " positivism " to which Morosoff adhered and from which he was unable to depart. His previous arguments led in quite another direction. Besides " spirits " there exist a number of phenomena altogether real to us, i.e. of usual and everyday occurrence, but absolutely inexplicable without the help of hypotheses which would relate these phenomena with the world of the fourth dimension. But we are too accustomed to these phenomena and do not notice their " miraculous character ", do not notice that we live in a world of perpetual miracle, in a world of the mysterious, the inexplicable and, above all, the unmeasurable.

Morosoff describes how miraculous our three-dimensional bodies would seem to the plane-beings, how these beings would not know whence our bodies come and whither they disappear like spirits appearing from an unknown world.

But in reality are we not beings just as fantastic and as changeable in our appearance for any stationary object, a stone or a tree ? Further, do we not possess the properties of " higher beings " for animals ? And are there no phenomena for us, for instance, all the manifestations of *life*, about which we do not know whence they come nor whither they go ; phenomena such as the appearance of a plant from a seed, the birth of living things, and the like ; and further, the phenomena of nature, thunderstorms, rain, spring, autumn, which we can neither explain nor interpret. Is not each of these phenomena of nature taken separately something of which we can feel only a little, touch only a part, like the blind men in the old Eastern fable who defined an elephant each in his own way ; one by its legs, another by its ears, a third by its tail.

Continuing Morosoff's reasonings concerning the relations between the world of three dimensions and the world of four dimensions, we have no grounds for looking for the latter only in the domain of " spiritualism ".

Let us take a living cell. It may be exactly equal in length, breadth and height to another, a dead cell. And still there is something in the living cell which is lacking in the dead one, something we are unable to measure.

We say that it is "vital force", try to explain the vital force as a kind of motion. But in reality we do not explain anything by this, but only give a name to a phenomenon which remains inexplicable.

According to some scientific theories vital force must be resolvable into physico-chemical elements, into simpler forces. But not one of these theories can explain how the one passes into the other and in what relation the one stands to the other. We are unable to express in a physico-chemical formula the simplest manifestations of life energy. And as long as we are unable to do so, we have no right, in a strictly logical sense, to regard vital processes as identical with physico-chemical processes.

We may accept philosophical "monism", but we have no reasons for accepting the physico-chemical monism imposed on us from time to time, which identifies vital and psychic processes with physico-chemical processes. Our mind may come in an abstract way to the conclusion of the unity of physico-chemical, vital, and psychic processes, but for science, for exact and concrete knowledge, these three classes of phenomena stand quite separate from one another.

For science, three classes of phenomena, mechanical force, vital force and psychic force, pass one into another only partially, and apparently without any fixed or calculable proportions. Therefore, scientists will be justified in explaining vital and psychic processes as a kind of motion only when they have found means of transforming motion into vital and psychic energy and vice versa, and of calculating such a transformation. This means that such an affirmation will be possible only when it is known what number of calories contained in a definite quantity of coal is necessary for starting the life of one cell, or how many atmospheres of pressure are necessary for the formation of one thought or one logical deduction. As long as these are not known, physical, biological and psychic phenomena, as studied by science, take place on different planes. Their unity can be surmised, but nothing can be affirmed positively.

If one and the same force acts in physico-chemical, vital and psychic processes, it may be supposed that it acts in different spheres only partly contiguous with one another.

If science really possessed knowledge of the unity of at least vital and physico-chemical phenomena, it would be able to create living organisms. In this expectation there is nothing extravagant. People construct machines and apparatus which are much more complicated externally than a simple one-cell organism. And yet they are unable to construct such an organism. This means that there is something in a living organism which does not exist in a lifeless machine. A living cell contains something which is lacking in a dead one. And we have every right to call this something equally inexplicable and unmeasurable. And in examining man we have good reasons for putting to ourselves the question: which part is bigger in him, the measurable or the unmeasurable?

"How can I answer your question" (about the fourth dimension), writes Morosoff in his letter to his fellow prisoners, "when I myself have no dimension in the direction indicated by you?"

But what real grounds has Morosoff for affirming so definitely that he has not this dimension?

Can he measure everything in himself? Two principal functions of man, *life* and *thought*, are in the domain of the unmeasurable.

We know so vaguely and so imperfectly what man really is, and we have in ourselves so much that is enigmatic and incomprehensible from the point of view of the geometry of three dimensions, that we have no reason to deny the fourth dimension in denying "spirits". On the contrary, we have ample grounds for looking for the fourth dimension precisely in ourselves.

And we have to confess to ourselves clearly and definitely that we do not know in the least what man really is. For us he is an enigma, and we must accept this enigma as such.

The "fourth dimension" promises to explain something in this enigma. Let us try to see what the "fourth dimension" can give us if we approach it with the old methods but without the old prejudices for or against spiritualism. Let us again imagine a world of plane-beings possessing only two dimensions, length and breadth, and inhabiting a flat surface.[1]

Let us imagine, on this surface, living beings having the shape of geometrical figures and capable of moving in two directions.

At the very beginning of the examination of the conditions of life of these flat beings we come at once face to face with a very interesting fact.

These beings will be able to move only in two directions on their plane. They will be unable to rise above this plane or to leave it. In the same way they will be unable to see or feel anything lying outside their plane. If one of these beings rises above the plane, he

[1] In these reasonings about imaginary worlds I shall partly follow Hinton's plan, but this does not mean that I share *all* Hinton's opinions.

will completely pass away from the world of other beings similar to it, will vanish, disappear—no one knows whither.

If we suppose that the organs of vision of these beings are situated on their edges, on their outer lines, then they will not be able to see the world lying outside their plane at all. They will see only lines lying on their plane. They will see each other not as they really are, i.e. in the shape of geometrical figures, but only in the form of lines. In the same way all the objects of their world will also appear to them as lines. And, what is very important, all lines, whether straight, curved, or with angles, or lying at different angles to the line of their edge, will appear to them alike; they will not be able to see any difference in the lines themselves. But at the same time, the lines will differ for them by strange properties which they will probably call the motion or the vibration of lines.

The centre of a circle will be entirely inaccessible to them. They will be quite unable to see it. In order to reach the centre of a circle a two-dimensional being will have to dig or cut his way through the mass of the flat figure having the thickness of one atom. The process of digging will appear to him as an altering of the line of the circumference.

If a cube is placed on his plane, then this cube will appear to him in the form of the four lines bounding the square touching his plane. Of the whole cube only this square will exist for him. He will be unable even to imagine the rest of the cube. The *cube* will not exist for him.

If several bodies come into contact with his plane, for a plane-being there will exist in each of them only one surface which has come into contact with his plane. This surface, that is, the lines bounding it, will appear to him as an object of his own world.

If through his space, that is, through his plane, there passes a multicoloured cube, the passage of the cube will appear to him as a gradual change in the colour of the lines bounding the square which lies on his plane.

If we suppose that the plane-being is made able to see with his flat side, the one facing our world, it is easy to imagine what a wrong conception of our world he will receive.

The whole universe will appear to him in the form of a plane. It is very probable that he will call this plane æther. Consequently, he will either completely deny all phenomena which take place outside his plane, or regard them as happening on his own plane, in his æther. Unable to explain on his plane all the phenomena observed by him, he may call them miraculous, lying above his understanding, beyond his space, in the "third dimension".

THE FOURTH DIMENSION 87

Having observed that the inexplicable events occur in a certain consecutiveness, in a certain dependence one upon another, and also probably in a dependence on some laws, the plane-being will cease to consider them miraculous and will attempt to explain them by means of more or less complicated hypotheses.

The appearance of the dim idea of another parallel plane will be for a plane-being the first step towards the right understanding of the universe. He will then imagine all the phenomena he is unable to explain on his own plane as occurring on that parallel plane. At this stage of development the whole of our world will appear to him as plane and parallel to his own plane. Neither relief nor perspective will exist for him as yet. A mountain landscape will appear to him as a flat photograph. His conception of the world will certainly be very poor, and full of errors. The big things will be taken for the small, and the small things for the big, and all together, whether near or far, will appear to him equally remote and inaccessible.

Having recognised that there is a world parallel to his plane world, the two-dimensional being will say that of the true nature of the relations between these two worlds he knows nothing.

In the parallel world there will be much that will appear inexplicable for a two-dimensional being. For instance a lever or a couple of wheels on an axle. Their action will appear quite inconceivable to the plane-being, whose conception of laws of motion is limited by motion on a plane. It is quite possible that this phenomenon will be considered supernatural and later will be called, in a more scientific way, " superphysical ".

In studying these superphysical phenomena the plane-being may stumble upon the idea that a lever, or wheels, contain something unmeasurable, but nevertheless existing.

From this there is only one step to the hypothesis of the third dimension. The plane-being will base this hypothesis precisely on inexplicable facts, such as the rotation of wheels. He may ask himself whether the inexplicable may not really be the unmeasurable, and then begin gradually to elucidate for himself the physical laws of three-dimensional space. But he will never be able to prove mathematically the existence of this third dimension, because all his geometrical speculations will proceed only on a plane, on two dimensions, and therefore he will project on a plane the results of his mathematical conclusions, in this way destroying all their meaning.

The plane-being will be able to obtain his first notion of the nature of the third dimension merely by means of logical reasonings and comparisons. That means that in examining the inexplicable that lies in the flat photograph (representing for him our world) the plane-being may arrive at the conclusion that many phenomena are inexplicable for him, because in the objects causing these phenomena there may be a certain *difference* which he does not understand and cannot measure.

Further, he may conclude that a real body must differ in some way from an imaginary one. And having once admitted the hypothesis of the third dimension, he will have to say that the real body, unlike the imaginary body, must possess at least a small third dimension.

In the same way the plane-being may come to the recognition that he must necessarily possess the third dimension.

After arriving at the conclusion that a real body of two dimensions cannot exist, that this is but an imaginary figure, the plane-being will have to say to himself that, since the third dimension exists, he must himself possess this third dimension, because otherwise, having only two dimensions, he would be but an imaginary figure, that is, exist only in somebody's mind.

The plane-being will reason in the following way: " If the third dimension exists, I am either a being of three dimensions or I do not exist in reality but exist only in somebody's imagination ".

In reflecting why he does not see his third dimension the plane-being may come upon the thought that his extension along the third dimension, just like the extension of other bodies along the third dimension, is very small. These reflections may bring the plane-being to the conclusion that for him the question of the third dimension is connected with the problem of small magnitudes.

In investigating the world in a philosophical way the plane-being will from time to time doubt the reality of everything surrounding him and the reality of himself.

He may then think that his conception of the world is wrong and that he does not even see it as it really is. Reasonings about things as they appear and about things as they are may follow from this. The plane-being may think that in the third dimension things must appear as they are, i.e. that he will see in the same things more than he saw in two dimensions.

Verifying all these reasonings from our point of view, that is, from the point of view of beings of three dimensions, we must recognise that all the conclusions of the plane-being are perfectly right and lead him to a right understanding of the world and to the cognition, though theoretical in the beginning, of the third dimension.

We may profit by the experience of the plane-being and try to find whether there is anything in the world towards which we are in the same relation as the plane-being is towards the third dimension.

In examining the physical conditions of the life of man we find in them an almost complete analogy with the conditions of life of the plane-being who begins to be aware of the third dimension.

We shall start by analysing our relation towards the " invisible ".

At first man considers the invisible as miraculous and supernatural. Gradually, with the evolution of knowledge, the idea of the miraculous becomes less and less necessary. Everything within the sphere accessible to observation (and unfortunately far beyond it) is regarded as existing according to certain definite laws, as the result of certain definite causes. But the causes of many phenomena remain hidden, and science is forced to limit itself to a classification of these inexplicable phenomena.

In studying the character and properties of the " inexplicable " in different branches of our knowledge, in physics and chemistry, in biology and in psychology, we can arrive at certain general conclusions concerning the character of the inexplicable. That means, we can formulate the problem as follows : is not the inexplicable a result of something " unmeasurable " for us which exists, first, in those things which, as it appears to us, we can measure fully, and second, in things which, as it appears to us, can have no measurement ?

We can think that this very inexplicability may be the result of the fact that we examine and attempt to explain, within the limits of three dimensions, phenomena that pass into the domain of a higher dimension. To put it differently, are we not in the position of the plane-being trying to explain as happening on a plane phenomena that take place in three-dimensional space ?

There is a great deal that confirms the probability of such a supposition.

It is quite possible that many inexplicable phenomena are inexplicable only because we wish to explain them on our plane, i.e. within our three-dimensional space, while really they occur outside our plane, in the domain of higher dimensions.

Having come to the conclusion that we are surrounded by the world of the unmeasurable, we must admit that, until now, we have had an entirely wrong conception of the objects of our world.

We knew before that we see things and represent them to ourselves not as they really are. Now we may say more definitely that we do not see in things that part of them which is unmeasurable for us, lying in the fourth dimension.

This last conclusion brings us to the idea of the difference between the imaginary and the real.

We saw that the plane-being, having arrived at the idea of the third dimension, must conclude that, if there are three dimensions, a real body of two dimensions cannot exist. A two-dimensional body would be only an imaginary figure, a section of a body of three dimensions or its projection in two-dimensional space.

Admitting the existence of the fourth dimension, we must recognise in the same way that if there are four dimensions, a real body of three dimensions cannot exist. A real body must possess at least a very small extension along the fourth dimension, otherwise it will be only an imaginary figure, the projection of a body of four dimensions in three-dimensional space, like a " cube " drawn on paper.

In this way we must come to the conclusion that there may exist a cube of three dimensions and a cube of four dimensions, and that only the cube of four dimensions will really, actually, exist.

Examining man from this point of view we come to very interesting deductions.

If the fourth dimension exists, one of two things is possible. Either we ourselves possess the fourth dimension, i.e. are beings of four dimensions, or we possess only three dimensions and in that case do not exist at all.

If the fourth dimension exists while we possess only three, it means that we have no real existence, that we exist only in somebody's imagination, and that all our thoughts, feelings and experiences take place in the mind of some other higher being, who visualises us. We are but products of his mind and the whole of our universe is but an artificial world created by his fantasy.

If we do not want to agree with this, we must recognise ourselves as beings of four dimensions.

At the same time we must recognise that our own fourth dimension, as well as the fourth dimension of the bodies surrounding us, is known and felt by us only very little and that we only guess its existence from observations of inexplicable phenomena.

Such blindness in relation to the fourth dimension may be caused by the fact that the fourth dimension of our own bodies and other objects of our world is too small and inaccessible to our organs of sense, or to the apparatus which widens the sphere of our observation, exactly in the same way as the molecules of our bodies and many other things are inaccessible to immediate observation. As regards objects possessing a greater extension in the fourth dimension, we feel them at times in certain circumstances, but refuse to recognise them as really existing.

These last considerations give us sufficient grounds for believing that, at least in our physical world, the fourth dimension must refer to the domain of small magnitudes.

The fact that we do not see in things their fourth dimension brings us again to the problem of the imperfection of our perceptions in general.

Even if we leave aside other defects of our perception and regard its activity only in relation to geometry, we shall have to admit that we see everything as very unlike what it really is.

We do not see bodies, we see nothing but surfaces, sides and lines. We never see a cube; we see only a small part of it, never see it from all the sides at once.

From the fourth dimension it must be possible to see the cube from all the sides at once and from within, as though from its centre.

The centre of a sphere is inaccessible to us. To reach it we must cut or dig our way through the mass of the sphere, i.e. act in exactly the same way as the plane-being with regard to the circle. The process of cutting through will in that case appear to us as a gradual change in the surface of the sphere.

The complete analogy of our relation to the sphere with the relation of the plane-being to the circle gives us grounds for thinking that in the fourth dimension, or along the fourth dimension, the centre of the sphere is as easily accessible as is the centre of the circle in the third dimension. In other words, we have a right to suppose that in the fourth dimension it is possible to reach the centre of the sphere from some region unknown to us, along some incomprehensible direction, the sphere itself remaining intact. The latter circumstance would appear to us a kind of miracle, but just as miraculous, to the plane-being, must appear the possibility of reaching the centre of the circle without disturbing the line of its circumference, without breaking up the circle.

Continuing to imagine further the properties of vision or perception in the fourth dimension, we shall have to recognise that not only in a geometrical sense, but also in many other senses, it is possible from the fourth dimension to see in objects of our world much more than we do see.

Prof. Helmholtz once said about our eye that if an optician sent him so badly made an instrument, he would never accept it.

Undoubtedly our eye does not see a great many things which exist. But if in the fourth dimension we see without the aid of such an imperfect instrument, we should be bound to see much more, that is, to see what is invisible for us now and to see everything without that net of illusions which veils the whole world from us and makes its outward aspect very unlike what it really is.

The question may arise why we should see in the fourth dimension without the aid of eyes, and what it means.

It will be possible to answer these questions definitely only when it is definitely known that the fourth dimension exists and when it is known what it really is. But so far it is possible to consider only what *might* be in the fourth dimension, and therefore there cannot be any final answers to these questions. Vision in the fourth dimension must be effected without the help of eyes. The limits of eyesight are known, and it is known that the human eye can never attain the perfection even of the microscope or telescope. But these instruments with all the increase of the power of vision which they afford do not bring us in the least nearer to the fourth dimension. So it may be concluded that vision in the fourth dimension must be something quite different from ordinary vision. But what can it actually be? Probably it will be something analogous to the " vision " by which a bird flying over Northern Russia " sees " Egypt, where it migrates for the winter; or to the vision of a carrier pigeon which " sees ", hundreds of miles away, its loft, from which it has been taken in a closed basket; or to the vision of an engineer making the first calculations and first rough drawings of a bridge, who " sees " the bridge and the trains passing over it; or to the vision of a man who, consulting a time-table, " sees " himself arriving at the station of departure and his train arriving at its destination.

Now, having outlined certain features of the properties which vision in the fourth dimension should possess, we must endeavour to define more exactly what we know of the phenomena of that world.

Again making use of the experience of the two-dimensional being, we must put to ourselves the following question:—are all the " phenomena " of our world explicable from the point of view of physical laws?

There are so many inexplicable phenomena around us that merely by being too familiar with them we cease to notice their inexplicability, and, forgetting it, we begin to classify these phenomena, give them names, include them within different systems and, finally, even begin to deny their inexplicability.

Strictly speaking, all is equally inexplicable. But we are accustomed to regard some orders of phenomena as more explicable and other orders as less explicable. We put the less explicable into a special group, and create out of them a separate world, which is regarded as parallel to the " explicable ".

This refers first of all to the so-called " psychic world ", that is to the world of ideas, images and conceptions, which we regard as parallel to the physical world.

Our relation to the psychic, the difference which exists for us between the physical and the psychic, shows that psychic phenomena should be assigned to the domain of the fourth dimension.[1] In the history of human thought the relation to the psychic is very similar to the relation of the plane-being to the third dimension. Psychic phenomena are inexplicable on the "physical plane", therefore they are regarded as opposite to the physical. But their unity is vaguely felt, and attempts are constantly made to interpret psychic phenomena as a kind of physical phenomena, or physical phenomena as a kind of psychic phenomena. The division of concepts is recognised to be unsuccessful, but there are no means for their unification.

In the first place the psychic is regarded as quite separate from the body, as a function of the "soul", unsubjected to any physical laws. The soul lives by itself, and the body by itself, and the one is incommensurable with the other. This is the theory of naïve dualism or spiritualism. The first attempt at an equally naïve monism regards the soul as a direct function of the body. It is then said that "thought is a motion of matter". Such was the famous formula of Moleschott.

Both views lead into blind alleys. The first, because the obvious interdependence of physiological and psychic processes cannot be disregarded; the second, because motion still remains motion and thought remains thought.

The first view is analogous to the denial by the two-dimensional being of any physical reality in phenomena which happen outside his plane. The second view is analogous to the attempt to consider as happening on a plane phenomena which happen above it or outside it.

The next step is the hypothesis of a parallel plane on which all the inexplicable phenomena take place. But the theory of parallelism is a very dangerous thing.

The plane-being begins to understand the third dimension when he begins to see that what he considered parallel to his plane may actually be at different distances from it. The idea of relief and perspective will then appear in his mind, and the world and things will take for him the same form as they have for us.

We shall understand more correctly the relation between physical and psychic phenomena when we clearly understand that the psychic is not always parallel to the physical and may be quite independent of it. And parallels which are not always parallel are evidently subject to laws that are incomprehensible to us, to laws of the world of four dimensions.

[1] The expression "psychic" phenomena is used here in its only possible sense of psychological or mental phenomena, that is, those which constitute the subject of psychology. I mention this because in spiritualistic and theosophical literature the word "psychic" is used for the designation of supernormal or superphysical phenomena.

At the present day it is often said: we know nothing about the exact nature of the relations between physical and psychic phenomena; the only thing we can affirm and which is more or less established is that for every psychic process, thought or sensation there is a corresponding physiological process, which manifests itself in at least a feeble vibration in nerves and brain fibre and in chemical changes in different tissues. Sensation is defined as the consciousness of a change in the organs of sense. This change is a certain motion which is transmitted into brain centres, but in what way the motion is transformed into a feeling or a thought is not known.

The question arises: is it not possible to suppose that the physical is separated from the psychic by four-dimensional space, i.e. that a physiological process, passing into the domain of the fourth dimension, produces there effects which we call feeling or thought?

On our plane, i.e. in the world of motion and vibrations accessible to our observations, we are unable to understand or to determine thought, exactly in the same way as the two-dimensional being on his plane is unable to understand or to determine the action of a lever or the motion of a pair of wheels on an axle.

At one time the ideas of E. Mach, expounded chiefly in his book *Analysis of Sensations and Relations of the Physical to the Psychic*, were in great vogue. Mach absolutely denies any difference between the physical and the psychic. In his opinion all the dualism of the usual view of the world resulted from the metaphysical conception of the " thing in itself " and from the conception (an erroneous one according to Mach) of the illusory character of our cognition of things. In Mach's opinion we can perceive nothing wrongly. Things are always exactly what they appear to be. The concept of illusion must disappear entirely. Elements of sensations are physical elements. What are called " bodies " are only complexes of elements of sensations: light sensations, sound sensations, sensations of pressure, etc. Mental images are similar complexes of sensations. There exists no difference between the physical and the psychic: both the one and the other are built up of the same elements (of sensations). The molecular structure of bodies and the atomic theory are accepted by Mach only as symbols, and he denies them all reality.

In this way, according to Mach's theory, our psychic apparatus builds the physical world. A " thing " is only a complex of sensations.

But in speaking of the theories of Mach it is necessary to remember that the psychic apparatus builds only the " forms " of the world (i.e. makes the world such as we perceive it) out of something else which we shall never attain. The blue of the sky is unreal, the green of the meadows is also unreal; these "colours" belong to the reflected rays. But evidently there is something in the "sky", i.e. in the air of our atmosphere, which makes it appear blue, just as there is something in the grass of the meadow which makes it appear green.

Without this last addition a man might easily have said, on the basis of Mach's ideas: this apple is a complex of my sensations, therefore it only seems to exist, but does not exist in reality.

This would be wrong. The apple exists. And a man can, in a most real way, become convinced of it. But it is not what it appears to be in the three-dimensional world.

The psychic, as opposed to the physical or the three-dimensional, is very similar to what should exist in the fourth dimension, and we have every right to say that thought moves along the fourth dimension.

No obstacles or distances exist for it. It penetrates impenetrable objects, visualises the structure of atoms, calculates the chemical composition of stars, studies life on the bottom of the ocean, the customs and institutions of a race that disappeared tens of thousands of years ago. . . .

No walls, no physical conditions, restrain our fantasy, our imagination.

Did not Morosoff and his comrades fly in their imagination far beyond the bastions of Schlüsselburg?

Did not Morosoff himself, in his book, *Revelation in Tempest and Thunderstorm*, travel through space and time when, as he was reading Revelations in the Alexeivsky ravelin of the Petropavlovsky Fortress he saw thunder clouds scudding over the Isle of Patmos in the Greek Archipelago, at five o'clock in the afternoon of the 30th September in the year 395?

Do we not in sleep live in a fantastic fairy kingdom where everything is capable of transformation, where there is no stability belonging to the physical world, where one man can become another or two men at the same time, where the most improbable things look simple and natural, where events often occur in inverse order, from end to beginning, where we see the symbolical images of ideas and moods, where we talk with the dead, fly in the air, pass through walls, are drowned or burnt, die, and remain alive?

All this taken together shows us that we have no need to think that the spirits that appear or fail to appear at spiritualistic séances must be the only possible beings of four dimensions. We may have very good reason for saying that we are ourselves beings of four dimensions and are turned towards the third dimension with only one of our sides, i.e. with only a small part of our being. Only this part of us lives in three dimensions, and we are conscious only of this part as our body. The greater part of our being lives in the fourth dimension, but we are unconscious of this greater part of ourselves. Or it would be still more true to say that we live in a four-dimensional world, but are conscious of ourselves only in a three-dimensional world. This means that we live in one kind of conditions, but imagine ourselves to be in another.

The conclusions of psychology bring us to the same idea, but by a different road. Psychology comes, though very slowly, to the recognition of the possibility of awakening our consciousness, i.e. the possibility of a particular state of it, when it sees and feels itself in a real world having nothing in common with this world of things and phenomena—in a world of thoughts, mental images and ideas.

In discussing earlier the properties of the fourth dimension, I mentioned that the tessaract, that is, a^4, may be obtained by the movement of a cube in space, on the condition that all the points of the cube move.

Consequently if we suppose that from each point of the cube there is drawn a line which this movement must follow, the combination of these lines will then form the projection of a body of four dimensions. This body, that is the tessaract, as was found before, can be regarded as an infinite number of cubes growing, as it were, out of the first cube.

Let us see now whether we know of any examples of such motion, which implies the motion of all points of the given cube.

Molecular motion, that is, the motion of minute particles of matter which is increased by heating and lessened by cooling, is the most appropriate example of motion along the fourth dimension, in spite of all the erroneous ideas of physicists with regard to this motion.

In an article entitled "May we hope to see molecules?"[1] Prof. Goldgammer writes that, according to modern views, molecules are bodies the lineal section of which is something between one millionth and one ten-millionth part of a millimetre. It has been calculated that one milliardth part of a cubic millimetre, that is, one cubic microne, at a temperature of 0° C. and at normal pressure contains about 30 million molecules of oxygen. "Molecules move very fast; thus under normal conditions the majority of molecules of oxygen have the velocity of about 450 metres per second. Molecules do not disperse in all directions instantaneously in spite of their great velocities

[1] In the review *Naoutchnoye Slovo*, February, 1903.

only because they collide every moment with one another and because of this change the direction of their motion. Owing to this the path of a molecule has the aspect of a very entangled zigzag, and a molecule actually 'marks time', as it were, on one spot."

Leaving aside for the time the entangled zigzag and the theory of colliding molecules (Brownian movement), we must try to find what results are produced by molecular motion in the visible world.

In order to find an example of motion along the fourth dimension we have to find a motion whereby the given body would actually move and not remain in one place (or one state).

Examining all the observable kinds of motion we must admit that the *expansion* and *contraction* of bodies come nearest to the indicated conditions.

Expansion of gases, liquids and solids means that molecules retreat from one another. Contraction of solids, liquids and gases means that the molecules approach one another. The distance between them diminishes. There is space here and there are distances.

Is it not possible that this space lies in the fourth dimension?

A movement in this space means that all the points of the given geometrical body, that is, all the molecules of the given physical body, move.

The figure resulting from the movement of a cube in space when the cube expands or contracts will have the form of a cube, and we can imagine it as an infinite number of cubes.

Is it right to suppose that the assemblage of lines drawn from every point of a cube, interior as well as exterior, the lines along which the points approach one another or retreat from each other, constitutes the projection of a four-dimensional body?

In order to answer this it is necessary to determine what these lines are and what this direction is.

These lines connect all the points of the given body with its centre. Consequently the direction of the movement indicated will be from the centre along the radii.

In investigating the paths of the movements of the points (or molecules) of a body in the case of expansion and contraction, we find in them many interesting features.

We cannot see the distance between molecules. We cannot see it in the case of solids, liquids and gases because it is extremely small, and in the case of highly rarefied matter, as for instance that in Crookes tubes, where this distance is probably increased to the proportions perceptible for us or for our apparatus, we cannot see it because the particles themselves, the molecules, are too small to be accessible to our observation. In the above-mentioned article Prof.

Goldgammer states that given certain conditions molecules could be photographed if they could be made luminous. He writes that when the pressure in Crookes tubes is reduced to one-millionth part of an atmosphere one microne will contain only 30 molecules of oxygen. If they were luminous they could be photographed on a screen.

To what extent this photographing is really possible, is another question. For the present argument, a molecule as a real quantity in relation to a physical body can represent a point in its relation to a geometrical body.

All bodies must necessarily consist of molecules; consequently they must possess a certain, though a very small, dimension of inter-molecular space. Without this we cannot conceive a real body, and can conceive only imaginary geometrical bodies. A real body consists of molecules and possesses a certain inter-molecular space.

This means that the difference between a cube of three dimensions, a^3, and a cube of four dimensions, a^4, will be that a cube of four dimensions consists of molecules, whereas a cube of only three dimensions in reality does not exist and is only a projection of a four-dimensional body in three-dimensional space.

In expanding or contracting, that is, in moving along the fourth dimension, if the preceding arguments are admitted, a cube or sphere remains for us all the time a cube or sphere, changing only in size. Hinton quite rightly observed in one of his books that the passing of a cube of higher dimension transversely to our space would appear to us as a change in the properties of the matter of the cube before us. He also says that the idea of the fourth dimension ought to have arisen from observation of a series of progressively growing or diminishing spheres or cubes. This last idea brings him quite near to the right definition of motion in the fourth dimension.

One of the clearest and most comprehensible forms of motion in the fourth dimension in this sense is growth, the principle of which lies in expansion. It is not difficult to explain why it is so. Every motion within the limits of three-dimensional space is at the same time a motion in time. Molecules or points of an expanding cube do not return to their former place on contraction. They trace a certain curve, returning, not to the point of time at which they started, but to another. And if we suppose that generally they do not return, the distance between them and the original point of time will continually increase. Let us imagine the internal motion of a body in the course of which its molecules, having retreated from one another, do not approach one another again, but the distance between them is filled up with new molecules, which in their turn move asunder and make room for new ones. Such an internal motion of a body would be its growth, at least a geometrical scheme of growth. If we compare a little green apple just formed from the ovary with a large red fruit we shall realise that the molecules composing the ovary could not create the apple while moving only in three-dimensional space. They need in addition to this a continuous motion in time, a continuous deviation into the space which lies outside the three-dimensional sphere. The apple is separated from the ovary by time. From this point of view the apple represents three or four months' motion of molecules along the fourth dimension. If we imagine the whole of the way from the ovary to the apple, we shall see the direction of the fourth dimension, that is, the mysterious fourth perpendicular—the line perpendicular to all three perpendiculars of our space and parallel to none of them.

On the whole Hinton stands so near to the correct solution of the problem of the fourth dimension that he sometimes guesses the place of the "fourth dimension" in life, although he cannot determine this place exactly. Thus he says that the symmetry of the structure of living organisms can be explained only by the movement of their particles along the fourth dimension.

Everybody knows, says Hinton,[1] the means of obtaining on paper, images resembling living insects. A few blots of ink are splashed on a piece of paper and the sheet is folded in two. A very complicated symmetrical image is obtained, resembling a fantastic insect. If a whole series of these figures were seen by a man quite unacquainted with the method of their production, then, thinking purely logically, he would have to conclude that they had originated from folding the paper in two, that is to say, that their symmetrically disposed points have been in contact. In the same way, in examining and studying structural forms of organised beings which very strongly resemble the figures on paper obtained by the above-described method, we may conclude that these symmetrical forms of insects, leaves, birds and other animals are produced by means of a process similar to this folding. And we may explain the symmetrical structure of organised beings, if not by folding in two in four-dimensional space, at any rate by a disposition in a manner similar to the folding of the smallest particles from which they are built up.

There exists indeed in nature a very interesting phenomenon, which gives us perfectly correct diagrams of the fourth dimension. It is only necessary to know how to read these diagrams. They are seen in the fantastically varied but always symmetrical shapes of snow-

[1] *The Fourth Dimension*, 2nd edition, 1921, pp. 18, 19.

flakes, and also in the designs of the flowers, stars, ferns and lacework which frost makes on window panes. Drops of water settling from the air on to a cold pane, or on to the ice already formed upon it, begin instantaneously to freeze and expand, leaving traces of their motion along the fourth dimension in the shape of intricate designs. These frost drawings on window panes, as well as the designs of snow-flakes, are figures of the fourth dimension, the mysterious a^4. The motion of a lower figure to obtain a higher one, as imagined in geometry, is here actually realised, and the resulting figure, in effect, represents the trace left by the motion of the lower figure, because the frost preserves all the stages of the expansion of freezing drops of water.

Forms of living bodies, living flowers, living ferns, are created according to the same principles, though in a more complex order. The outline of a tree gradually spreading into branches and twigs is, as it were, a diagram of the fourth dimension, a^4.

FIG. 1.—A diagram of the Fourth Dimension in Nature.

Leafless trees in winter or early spring often present very complicated and extraordinarily interesting diagrams of the fourth dimension. We pass them without noticing them because we think that a tree exists in three-dimensional space. Similar wonderful diagrams can be seen in the designs of sea-weeds, flowers, young shoots, certain seeds, etc., etc. Sometimes it is sufficient to magnify them a little in order to see the secrets of the " Great Laboratory " that are hidden from our eye.

Some very remarkable illustrations of the above statements may be found by the reader in Prof. K. Blossfeldt's book on art-forms in nature.[1]

Living organisms, the bodies of animals and human beings, are built on the principles of symmetrical motion. In order to understand these principles let us take a simple schematic example of symmetrical motion. Let us imagine a cube composed of 27 small cubes, and let us imagine this cube as expanding and contracting. During the process of expansion all the 26 cubes lying round the central cube will retreat from it and on contraction will approach it again. For the sake of convenience in reasoning and in order to increase the likeness of the cube to a body consisting of molecules, let us suppose that the cubes have no dimension, that they are nothing but points. In other words, let us take only the centres of the 27 cubes and imagine them connected by lines both with the centre and with each other.

Visualising the expansion of this cube, composed of 27 cubes, we may say that in order to avoid colliding with another cube and hindering its motion, each of these cubes must move away from the centre, that is to say, along the line which connects its centre with the centre of the central cube.

This is the first rule.

In the course of expansion and contraction molecules move along the lines which connect them with the centre.

Further, we see in our cube that the lines connecting the 26 points with the centre are not all equal. The lines drawn to the centre from the centres of the corner cubes are longer than the lines drawn to the centre from the centres of the cubes lying in the middle of the sides of the large cube.

If we suppose that the inter-molecular space is doubled by expansion, then all the lines connecting the 26 points with the centre are at the same time doubled in length. The lines are not equal; therefore molecules move with unequal speed, some of them faster, and some slower; those further removed from the centre move faster, those lying nearer the centre move slower.

From this we may deduce a second rule.

The speed of the motion of molecules in the expansion and contraction of a body is proportional to the length of the lines which connect these molecules with the centre.

Observing the expansion of the big cube, we see that the distances

---

[1] *Art Forms in Nature*, by Prof. Karl Blossfeldt, with an introduction by Karl Nierendorf (London: A. Zwemmer, 1929).

between *all* the 27 cubes are increased proportionally to the former distances.

If we designate by the letter a lines connecting the 26 points with the centre, and by the letter b lines connecting the 26 points with one another, then, having constructed several triangles inside the expanding and contracting cube, we shall see that lines b are lengthened proportionally to the lengthening of lines a.

From this we deduce a third rule.

In the process of expansion the distance between molecules increases proportionally to the increase of their distance from the centre.

This means therefore that the points that were at an equal distance from the centre will remain at an equal distance from it, and two points that were at an equal distance from a third point will remain at an equal distance from it.

Moreover, if we look upon this motion not from the centre, but from any one of the points, it will appear to us that this point is the centre from which the expansion proceeds, that is to say, it will appear that all the other points retreat from or approach this point, preserving their former relation to it and to each other, while this point itself remains stationary. "The centre is everywhere!"

The laws of symmetry in the structure of living organisms are based on this last rule. But living organisms are not built by expansion alone. The element of movement in time enters into it. In the course of growth each molecule traces a curve resulting from the combination of two movements, movement in space and movement in time. Growth proceeds in the same direction, along the same lines, as expansion. Therefore the laws of growth must be analogous to the laws of expansion. The conditions of expansion, that is, the *third rule*, ensure the most rigorous symmetry in freely expanding bodies, because if points which were originally at an equal distance from the centre continue always to remain at an equal distance from it, the body will grow symmetrically.

In the figure produced by the ink spread on a sheet of paper folded in two, the symmetry of all the points was obtained because the points on one side came into contact with the points on the other side. To each point on one side there corresponded a point on the other side and, when the paper was folded, these points touched one another. From the third rule formulated above it must follow that between the opposite points of a four-dimensional body there exists some relation, some affinity, which we have not hitherto noticed. To each point there corresponds as it were one or several others linked with it in some way unintelligible to us. That is, this point is unable to move independently; its movement is connected with the movement of other corresponding points, which occupy positions analogous to its own in the expanding and contracting body. And these points are precisely the points opposite to it. It is, as it were, linked with them, linked in the fourth dimension. An expanding body appears to be folded in different ways and this establishes a certain strange connection between its opposite points.

Let us try to examine the way in which the expansion of the simplest figure is effected. We will take this figure not in space even, but on

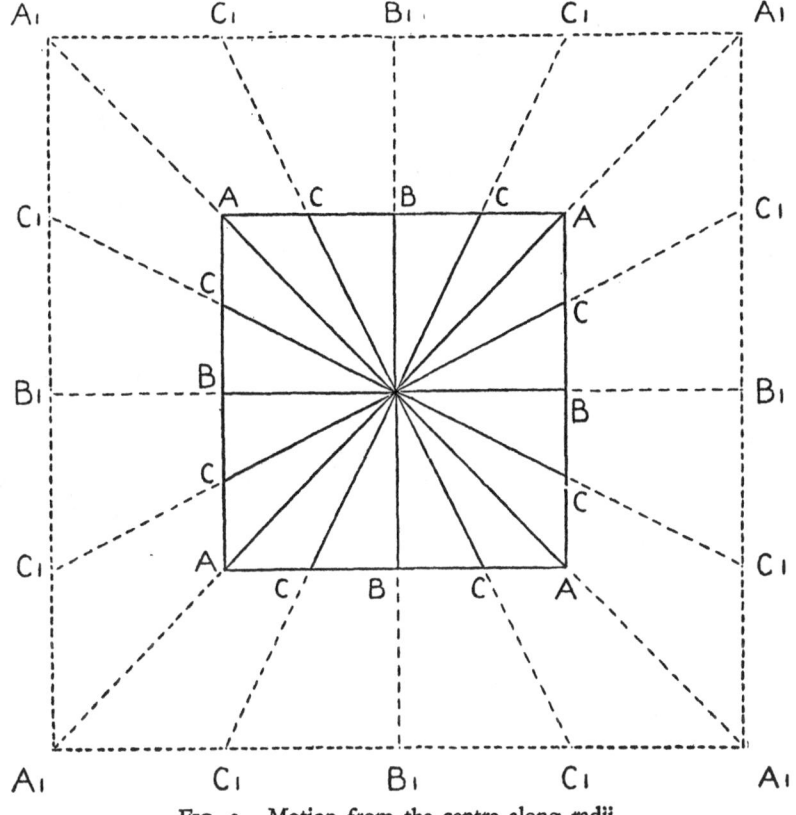

FIG. 2.—Motion from the centre along radii.

a plane. We will take a square. We will connect the four points at its angles with the centre. Then we will connect with the centre points lying in the middle of the sides, and then points lying half-way between them. The first four points, that is, those lying at the angles, we will call points A; the four points lying in the middle of the sides of the square we will call points B, and finally the points lying also on the sides of the square between A and B (there will be eight of them) we will call points C.

The points A, the points B and the points C lie at different distances from the centre, and therefore on expansion they must move with unequal speed, all the time preserving their relation to the centre. At the same time all the points A are connected among themselves, just as the points B are connected among themselves and as the points C are connected among themselves. Between the points of each group there is a strange inner connection. They must remain at *equal* distances from the centre.

Let us now suppose that the square is expanding, or in other words that all the points, A, B and C retreat from the centre along radii. As long as the expansion of the figure proceeds unhindered, the movement of the points will follow the above-mentioned rules, and the figure will remain a square and preserve a most exact symmetry. But let us suppose that suddenly some obstacle has arisen on the path of the motion of one of the points C, forcing this to stop. In such a case there are two possible alternatives. Either all the other points C will continue to move as if nothing had happened, or they also will stop. If they continue to move, the symmetry of the figure will be broken. If they stop, it will mean a strict observance of the deduction from rule 3, according to which points at an equal distance from the centre must on expansion remain at an equal distance from it. In fact if all the points C, obeying the mysterious affinity which exists between them and the point C which met with an obstacle, stop, while points A and B continue to move, then the square will be transformed into a regular, perfectly symmetrical star. It is quite possible that a similar thing happens in the process of the growth of plants and living organisms. Let us take a more complicated figure, in which the centre from which the expansion starts is not a point, but a line, and in which the points retreating from the centre on expansion are disposed on both sides of that line. An analogous expansion will then produce not a star, but something resembling a dentate leaf. If we take this figure as lying in three-dimensional space instead of on a plane and suppose that the centres from which the expansion develops lie not on one but on several axes, we shall obtain on expansion a figure which may resemble a living body with symmetrical limbs, etc.; and if we suppose a movement of the atoms of this figure in time, we shall obtain the "growth" of a living body.

Laws of growth, that is, of motion originating in the centre and proceeding along radii in expansion and contraction, establish a theory which may explain the causes of the symmetrical structure of living bodies.

The definition of states of matter in physics has been becoming more and more conditional. At one time there was an attempt to add to the three generally known states—solid, liquid and gaseous—a fourth, "radiant matter", as the greatly rarefied gases in Crookes tubes were called. Then there exists a theory which considers the colloidal (gelatinous) state of matter as an independent state of matter, different from solid, liquid and gaseous. Organised matter, from the point of view of this theory, is a kind of colloidal matter or is formed from the colloidal matter. The concept of matter in these states was opposed to the concept of energy. Then appeared the electronic theory, in which the concept of matter became very little different from the concept of energy; later came various theories of the structure of the atom, which introduced many new ideas into the concept of matter.

But in this domain more than any other scientific theories differ from ordinary life conceptions. For a direct orientation in the world of phenomena it is necessary for us to distinguish matter from energy, and it is necessary to distinguish the three states of matter—solid, liquid and gaseous. At the same time it must be recognised that even these three states of matter known to us are distinguished by us clearly and indisputably only in their most "classical" forms, like a piece of iron, the water in a river, the air which we breathe. But the transitional forms overlap and are not clear. Therefore very often we do not know exactly when one state passes into the other, cannot draw a definite line of demarcation between the states of matter, cannot say when a solid has been transformed into a liquid, when a liquid has been transformed into gas. We presume that different states of matter depend on a different cohesion of molecules, on the speed and properties of molecular motion, but we distinguish these states only by their external traits, which are very inconstant and often become intermixed.

It can be said definitely that the finer the state of matter the more energetic it is considered to be, that is to say, containing as it were less substance and more motion. If matter is opposed to time, it will be possible to say that each finer state contains more time and less matter than a coarser state.

There is more "time" in a liquid than in a solid; there is more "time" in gas than in liquid.

If we accept the possibility of the existence of still finer states of matter, they should be more energetic than those recognised by physics; they should contain, according to the above, more time and less space, still more motion and still less substance.

The logical necessity of energetic states of matter has long been accepted in physics and is proved by very clear reasoning.

... What after all is substance? ... [1] The definition of substance has never been very clear and has become still less clear since the discoveries of modern science. Is it possible, for instance, to define as a substance the mysterious agent to which physicists have recourse for the explanation of phenomena of heat and light? This agent, this medium, this mechanism—call it what you like—nevertheless exists, for it manifests itself in indisputable action. Besides, it is deprived of the qualities without which it is difficult to imagine a substance. It has no weight, and possibly it has no mass; it does not produce any direct impression on any one of our organs of sense; in a word it does not possess a single feature which would indicate what was formerly called " material ". On the other hand it is not a spirit, at least nobody has ever thought of calling it that. But does it mean that it is necessary to deny its reality only because it cannot be classified as substance?

Is it necessary in the same way and for the same reason to deny the reality of the mechanism by means of which gravitation is transmitted into the depths of space with a velocity infinitely greater than the velocity of light,[2] which Laplace considered instantaneous? The great Newton considered it impossible to do without this agent. He to whom belongs the discovery of universal gravitation wrote to Bentley: " That Gravity should be innate, inherent and essential to Matter, so that one Body may act upon another at a Distance thro' a Vacuum, without the Mediation of anything else, by and through which their Action and Force may be conveyed from one to another, is to me so great an Absurdity, that I believe no Man who has in philosophical Matters a competent Faculty of thinking, can ever fall into it. Gravity must be caused by an Agent acting constantly according to certain Laws; but whether this Agent be material or immaterial, I have left to the Consideration of my Readers " (3rd letter to Bentley, 25th February, 1692).

The difficulty of allotting a place to these agents is so great that certain physicists, for example Hirn, who has unfolded this idea in his book, *Structure of Celestial Space*, consider it possible to imagine a new class of agents which occupy a position, so to speak, in the middle, between the material and the spiritual order and serve as a great source to the forces of nature. This class of agents, called dynamic by Hirn, from the conception of which he excludes all idea of mass and weight, serves, as it were, to establish relations, to provoke actions over a distance between different parts of matter.

The theory of Hirn's dynamic agents is based upon the following: We could never determine what matter and force really were, but in any case we always considered them opposite to one another, that is to say, we could define matter only as something opposite to force and force as something opposite to matter. But now the old views of matter as something solid and opposite to energy have considerably

[1] *Essais sur la philosophie des sciences.* C. de Freycinet (Gauthier Villars & Fils, éditeurs). Paris, 1896, pp. 300-2.
[2] This was written in the nineties of last century.

changed. A physical atom, formerly regarded as indivisible, is now recognised to be complex, composed of electrons. Electrons, however, are not material particles in the usual meaning of the word. They are better defined as moments of manifestation of energy, moments or elements of force. To put it in a different way, electrons, representing the smallest divisions of matter possible, are at the same time the smallest divisions of force. Electrons can be positive or negative. It is possible to think that the difference between matter and force consists simply in different combinations of positive and negative electrons. In one combination they produce on us the impression of matter, in another combination, the impression of force. From this point of view the difference between matter and force, which constitutes so far the basis of our view of nature, does not exist. Matter and force are one and the same thing or, rather, different manifestations of one and the same thing. In any case there is no essential difference between matter and force, and the one must pass into the other. From this point of view matter is nothing but condensed energy. And if it is so, then it is quite natural that degrees of condensation might be different. This theory explains how Hirn was unable to conceive half-material, half-energetic agents. Fine rarefied states of matter must in fact occupy a middle position between matter and force.

In his book *Unknown Forces of Nature*, C. Flammarion wrote: "Matter is not at all what it appears to our senses, to touch or vision. . . . It represents one single whole with energy and is the manifestation of the motion of invisible and imponderable elements. The Universe has a dynamic character. Guillaume de Fontenay gives the following explanation of the dynamic theory. In his opinion matter is in no way the inert substance it is usually considered to be."

> Let us take a carriage wheel and place it horizontally on the axle. The wheel is not moving. Let us take a rubber ball and make it fall between the spokes. Now let us make the wheel move slightly. The ball will fairly often hit the spokes and rebound. If we increase the rotation of the wheel the ball will not pass through it at all; the wheel will become for it a kind of impenetrable disc. We may make a similar experiment placing the wheel vertically and pushing a rod through it. A bicycle wheel will serve the purpose well, as its spokes are thin. When the wheel is stationary, the rod will pass through it nine times out of ten. When in motion the wheel will repel the rod more and more often. When the speed of its motion is increased it will become impenetrable, and all efforts at piercing it will strike as against steel armour.[1]

---

[1] Camille Flammarion, *Les forces naturelles inconnues*. Paris, 1927 (E. Flammarion, éditeur), p. 568.

Now having examined in the world surrounding us all that answers to the physical conditions of a higher dimensional space, we may put the question more definitely: What is the fourth dimension?

We have seen that it is impossible to prove its existence mathematically or to determine its properties and above all to define its position in relation to our world. Mathematics admits only the possibility of the existence of higher dimensions.

At the very beginning, when defining the idea of the fourth dimension, I pointed out that if it existed, it would mean that besides the three perpendiculars known to us there must exist a fourth. And this in its turn would mean that from any point of our space a line can be traced in a direction unknown and unknowable for us, and further that quite close, side by side with us, but in an unknown direction, there lies some other space which we are unable to see and into which we cannot pass.

I explained later why we are unable to see this space and I determined that it must lie not side by side with us in an unknown direction, but inside us, inside the objects of our world, inside our atmosphere, inside our space. However, this is not the solution of the whole problem, although it is a necessary stage on the way to this solution, because the fourth dimension *is not only inside us*, but we ourselves are inside it, that is, in the space of four dimensions.

I mentioned before that " spiritualists " and " occultists " of different schools often use the expression " fourth dimension " in their literature, assigning to the fourth dimension all phenomena of the " astral sphere ".

The " astral sphere " of the occultists which permeates our space is an attempt to find a place for phenomena which do not fit into our space. And consequently it is to a certain extent that continuation of our world inwards which we require.

The " astral sphere " from an ordinary point of view may be defined as the *subjective world*, projected outside us and taken for the *objective world*. If anybody actually succeeded in establishing the objective existence of even a portion of what is called " astral ", it would be the world of the fourth dimension.

But the very concept of the " astral sphere " or " astral matter " has changed many times in occult teachings.

On the whole, if we take the views of " occultists " of different schools on nature, we shall see that they are based upon the recognition of the possibility of studying conditions of existence other than our physical ones, and of using the knowledge of these other conditions of existence for the purpose of influencing our physical conditions. " Occult " theories generally start from the recognition of one basic substance, the knowledge of which provides *a key* to the knowledge of the mysteries of nature. But the concept of this substance is not definite. Sometimes it is understood as a *principle*, as a *condition of existence*, and sometimes as *matter*. In the first instance the basic substance contains in itself the roots and causes of things and events; in the second instance the basic substance is the primary matter from which everything else is obtained. The first concept is of course much more subtle and is the result of more elaborate philosophical thought. The second concept is more crude and is in most cases a sign of the decline of thought, a sign of an ignorant handling of difficult and profound ideas.

Philosopher-alchemists called this fundamental substance " Spiritus Mundi "—the spirit of the world. But alchemists—*seekers after gold*—considered it possible to put the spirit of the world into a crucible and subject it to chemical manipulations.

This should be kept in mind in order to understand the " astral hypotheses " of modern theosophists and occultists. Saint-Martin and, later, Eliphas Lévi still understood the " astral light " as a *principle*, as conditions of existence other than our physical conditions. But in the case of modern spiritualists and theosophists " astral light " has been transformed into " astral matter ", which can be *seen* and even photographed. The theory of " astral matter " is based on the hypothesis of " fine states of matter ". The hypothesis of fine states of matter was still possible in the last decades of the old physics, but it is difficult to find a place for it in modern physico-chemical thought. On the other hand, modern physiology deviates further and further from physico-mechanical explanations of vital processes and comes to the recognition of the enormous influence of *traces of matter*, that is, of imponderable and chemically indefinable matters, which are nevertheless clearly seen by the results of their presence, such as " hormones ", " vitamines ", " internal secretions " and so on.

Therefore, in spite of the fact that the hypothesis of fine states of matter does not stand in any relation whatever to new physics I shall attempt here to give a short exposition of the " astral theory ".

According to this theory particles resulting from the division of physical atoms produce a kind of special fine matter—" astral matter "—unsubjected to the action of the majority of physical forces, but subjected to the action of forces not affecting physical matter. Thus this " astral matter " is subjected to the action of psychic energy, will, feelings and desires, which are real forces in the astral sphere. This means that man's will, and also his sense reactions and emotional impulses, act upon " astral matter " just as physical energy acts upon physical bodies.

Further, the transformation into the astral state of physical matter composing visible bodies and objects is recognised as possible. This is *dematerialisation*, that is, from the physical point of view, a complete disappearance of physical objects no one knows where without trace or remains. Also, the reverse process, that is, the transformation of astral matter into the physical state or into physical matter is recognised as possible. This is *materialisation*, that is, the appearance of things, objects and even living beings from no one knows where.

Moreover, it is recognised as possible that matter which enters into the composition of a physical body, after having been transformed into the astral state, may " return " to the physical state in another form. Thus one metal, having been transformed into the astral state, may " return " in the form of another metal. In this way alchemical processes are explained by the temporary transference of some body, most often some metal, into an astral state where matter is subject to the action of will (or of spirits) and may change entirely under the influence of this will and reappear in the physical world *as another metal*; thus iron can change into gold. It is recognised as possible to accomplish this transformation of matter from one state into another and the transformation of one body into another by means of mental influence, assisted by certain rituals, etc. Further it is considered possible to see in the astral sphere events which have not yet happened in the physical sphere, but which must happen and must influence both the past and the future.

All this taken together makes up the content of what is called magic.

Magic, in the usual understanding of this word, means the capacity to accomplish what cannot be accomplished by ordinary physical means. Such would be, for instance, the power to influence psychically people and objects at a distance, to see people's actions and to know their thoughts, to make them disappear from our world and appear in unexpected places; the capacity to change one's appearance and even one's physical nature, to transfer oneself in some inconceivable way to great distances, to pass through walls, etc.

" Occultists " explain all such acts by the knowledge of the properties of the " astral sphere " possessed by magicians and their ability to act mentally upon astral matter and through it upon physical matter. Certain kinds of " sorcery " can be explained by the imparting of special properties to inanimate objects. This is attained by means of influencing physically their " astral matter ", by a special kind of psychic magnetisation of them; in this way magicians could impart to objects any properties they chose, make them execute their will, bring good or evil to other people, warn them against impending disasters, give force or take force away. To such magical practices belongs, for instance, the "blessing of water", which has now become nothing but a rite in Christian and Buddhist religious services. Originally it was an operation undertaken for the purpose of saturating water psychically with certain radiations or emanations with the aim of endowing it with the desired qualities, curative or other.

In theosophical and modern occult literature there are many very picturesque descriptions of the astral sphere. But no proofs of the objective existence of the astral sphere are anywhere given.

"Spiritualistic" proofs, that is, phenomena at séances, or "mediumistic" phenomena in general, "communications", etc., ascribed to spirits, that is, to disincarnated souls, are in no sense proofs, because all these phenomena can be explained much more simply. In the chapter on dreams I point out the possible meaning of spiritualistic phenomena as the results of impersonation. Theosophical explanations based upon "clairvoyance" require first of all proof of the existence of "clairvoyance", which remains unproved in spite of the number of books the authors of which have described what they attained or what they found by means of clairvoyance.

It is not generally known that in France there exists a prize established many years ago, which offers a considerable sum of money to anybody who would read a letter in a closed envelope. The prize remains unclaimed.

Both the spiritualistic and the theosophical theories suffer from one common defect which explains why "astral" hypotheses remain always the same and receive no proofs. "Space" and "time" are taken both in spiritualistic and in theosophical astral theories in exactly the same way as in the old physics, that is, separately from one another. "Disincarnated spirits" or "astral beings" or thought forms are taken *spatially* as bodies of the fourth dimension, but *in time* as physical bodies. In other words they remain in the same time conditions as physical bodies. And it is precisely this that is impossible. If "fine states of matter" produce bodies of different spatial existence, these bodies must have a different time existence. But this idea does not enter into theosophical or spiritualistic thought.

In this chapter there has been collected only the historical material relating to the study of the "fourth dimension", or rather that part of the historical material which brings one nearer to the solution of the problem or at least to its more exact formulation.

In this book, in the chapter "A New Model of the Universe", I show how the problems of "space-time" are connected with the problems of the structure of matter, and consequently the structure of the world, and how they lead to a right understanding of the *real* world, avoiding a whole series of unnecessary hypotheses, both pseudo-occult and pseudo-scientific.

1908–1929.

This is the end of this publication.

Any remaining blank pages are for our book binding requirements and are blank on purpose.

To search thousands of interesting publications like this one, please remember to visit our website at:

http://www.kessinger.net

CPSIA information can be obtained
at www.ICGtesting.com
Printed in the USA
LVHW061412030323
740863LV00005B/227